A Baby's Garden

A Baby's Garden

Introducing Your Baby to the Joys of the Garden

by Elizabeth St. Cloud Muse

Illustrated by Eva Saull

LITTLE, BROWN AND COMPANY

BOSTON NEW YORK LONDON

First Edition

ISBN 0-316-60873-4

Book design by Jo Anne Metsch

10 9 8 7 6 5 4 3 2 1

SC-CHINA

Printed in Hong Kong

These are the gardening adventures of

. . . .

Contents

Introduction

This book will open the wonders of the garden to the little eyes, ears, hands, and nose of your baby. Every day, you can take your infant into the garden for an adventure in sight, sound, texture, and scent. You can capture your wonderful memories on the pages of this journal and keep them for years to come.

Exploring the garden with your baby is a rewarding experience. As parents, we are responsible for guiding our children through the world, with its wonders and dangers. Of course, one of the ways babies begin to explore the world is by putting things in their mouths! In our garden, I have taught my son that nothing should be put in his mouth and that everything is "yucky." He learned fast. Later on, when he is old enough to know what is safe to eat and what is not, he can taste our garden's fruits. For now, however, we will work with the other four senses. I hope that your gardening experience with your baby is as rewarding as mine has been.

Birds

Babies love to watch and listen to birds as they fly from branch to branch and talk to one another across the garden. Each bird has a favorite kind of food and time of year that it can most often be seen. Place a bird feeder near your favorite bench or in a nearby tree. As you and your infant spend more time together in the garden, you will recognize many different kinds of birds, their favorite places to perch, and the wonderful songs they sing. Hang a bird feeder just outside your window and bring the birds even closer to your home. On chilly days, snuggle with your baby in a comfy chair, look out at all the colorful birds, and talk about each one. Mourning doves, sparrows, and chickadees will all come for a visit.

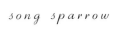 song sparrow

 hummingbird

Bird	Date	Description of the Moment

 robin

mourning dove

goldfinch

chickadee

blue jay

Bird	Date	Description of the Moment

swallow

woodpecker

red-winged blackbird

Grass

Lay your infant on a blanket in the grass. When children are very small, they find the smell and feel of the grass all around simply wonderful. Babies love to be tickled under their chins and on their little feet with pieces of grass. As they get older and can support themselves with their arms, place them at the edge of a blanket. They will love pulling fistfuls of grass out of the ground. The sound of grass as it is ripped from the earth and the coarse feel of grass in little hands add to the delight. Before you know it, your baby will be crawling across the yard gathering grass stains and giggling in delight.

Dirt

In a special part of the garden, loosen the soil and create a place for your infant to sit and play. Babies love the feel of dirt. Your little one will grasp handfuls of soil and hold on tight, feeling the coolness and texture of the earth. Tiny hands covered in mud are a wonderful sight to see.

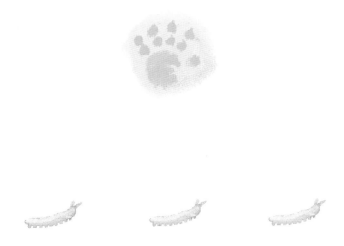

Muddy Hand Prints: Three Months

Muddy Hand Prints: Six Months

Muddy Hand Prints: Nine Months

Muddy Hand Prints: Twelve Months

Flowers

You can grow any number of flowers that both you and your baby will love, everything from sweet-smelling lilacs and vibrant daffodils to the crinkly petals of strawflowers and the smooth touch of a rosebud. Let your little one hold the flowers and feel the different textures and sizes of the petals. Babies can smell the flowers and enjoy their scents. Record your infant's favorite flowers from each season and save the vibrant petals by pressing them in the pages of this book.

FLOWERS IN THE GARDEN

Season

_____

tulip

primrose

rose

daisy

FLOWERS IN THE GARDEN

Season

---

daffodil

hyacinth

rhododendron

FLOWERS IN THE GARDEN
Season

_____

_____   _____

_____   _____

_____   _____

_____   _____

_____   _____

_____   _____

_____   _____

_____   _____

_____   _____

iris   *calla lily*   *gerbera daisy*

FLOWERS IN THE GARDEN

Season

_____

poppy

petunia

Wind

The sound of wind chimes through a garden is something that people of all ages treasure. Babies are no exception. Wind chimes can be found with the sweetest of melodies or the deepest of pitches. Place wind chimes where they can pick up a gentle breeze. Once babies learn the sound and see the wind chimes move, they will want to touch and make the music themselves. Hold them up close so they too can make the chimes sing.

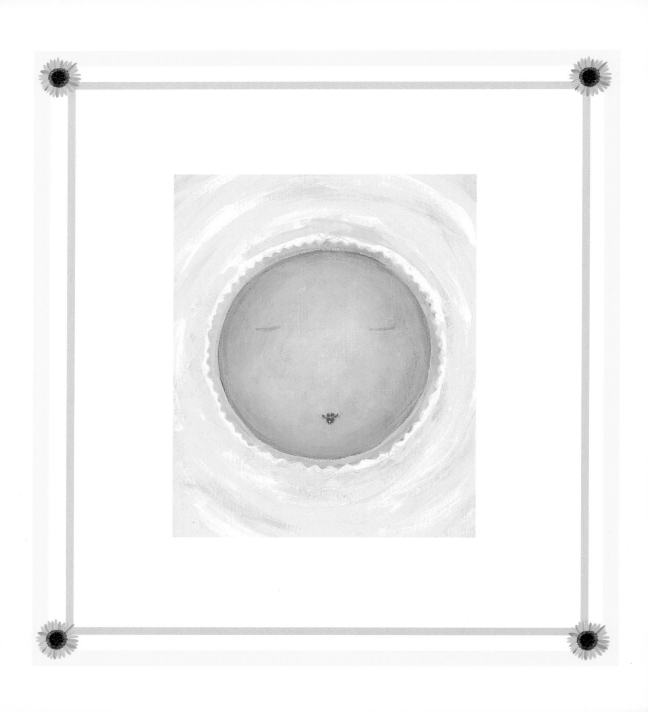

Shadows

Babies can distinguish between the light and dark that shadows cast. Place your infant on a light-colored blanket on the ground. With the sun behind you both, use your hands to cast a shadow. Show your baby the movement of the shadow on the blanket. Your baby will try to reach out and touch the shadow. As time goes by, your little one will turn around and make a remarkable discovery about where those shadows come from and want to join in the fun!

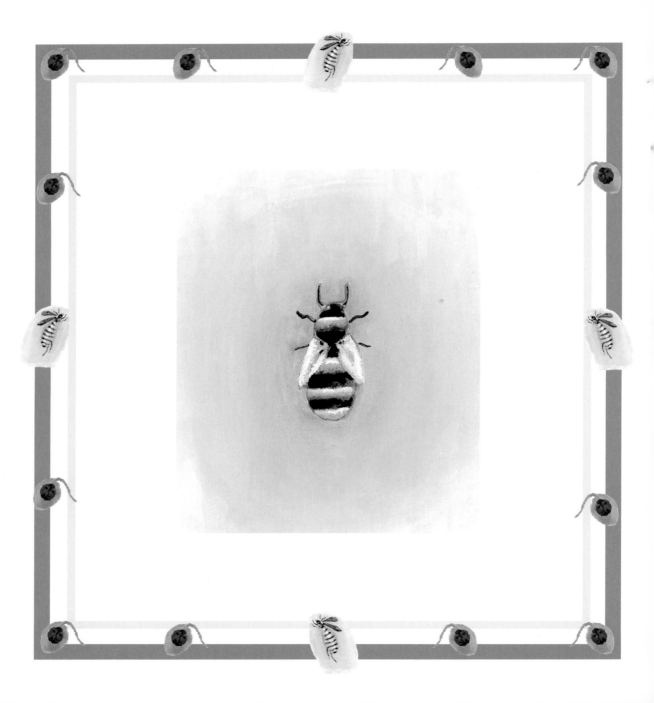

Bugs and Bees

The flowers and plants in your garden draw bees, butterflies, and other tiny winged creatures to your doorstep. Point out all the insects to your baby. Bumblebees, ladybugs, and butterflies all are brightly colored with their own distinct shapes and sizes. Infants delight in the sights and sounds of little bugs. Some creepy-crawly things bite and sting, so keep your distance and enjoy looking.

Herbs

A garden of any size can have fragrant herbs. Rosemary, mint, and any number of culinary plants can be grown right outside the kitchen door in large plots, window boxes, or small containers. Let your little one touch and smell the herbs you are growing. Each plant has a unique texture and scent. Not too long from now, your baby will appreciate the taste of each herb all the more, having enjoyed their fragrances in the garden early on.

HERBS

. . . .

_____

_____

_____

_____

_____

_____

_____

_____

_____

_____

sweet basil

parsley

garlic clove

HERBS

. . . .

borage

lavender

rosemary

Airplanes

Airplanes are one of the sights and sounds from the outside world that can be welcomed into the garden. Babies love to listen for airplanes and look to the sky to find them. You can help your infant spot a plane by pointing in its direction. By calling attention to the sound of the airplane before it becomes visible, babies learn to anticipate events and are happily rewarded when they see the plane flying through the air. Before you know it, your infant will be calling out loud and waving wildly every time an airplane goes over.

Leaves

The garden offers an amazing variety of leaves on its trees, bushes, and flowers. Each kind has a distinct size, color, and texture. In the spring, the leaves are soft and new, and the colors are fresh. As the year progresses through autumn, the colors will change and develop rich shades from yellow to brown to red. The texture will change from supple to crisp. Let your infant see and hold many different leaves. Your baby will delight in the sound of fall's leaves as they crunch between fingers. As the seasons change and your baby grows, you can keep special leaves tucked away to be shared and enjoyed another day.

oak

fruit

birch

pine

maple

magnolia

Chilly Days

When the air begins to cool and the smell of the coming winter is on the wind, your garden and your adventures will begin to change. On chilly mornings, look for the trails of ice that Jack Frost has left on your windows. With your baby's fingers, trace the frost's delicate lines and swirls before the sun melts them away. A stroll together in the garden will reveal blankets of ice crystals thinly covering the grass. The grass that was once warm to the touch now feels cold to little hands. For the first time, your baby can see your breath as you lean down and whisper, "I love you."

Quiet Time

Every day steal away ten minutes for yourself and your baby in the garden. This time is a shared moment to see and listen to the world around you. It is amazing how much peace ten minutes can bring when you sit in a favorite chair or lie on a soft blanket and just enjoy being outside in the fresh air for a quiet moment together. Sometimes the simplest things are the most rewarding.

Special Memories

Special Memories